Original title:
Moments of Magic

Author: Julian Prescott
ISBN HARDBACK: 978-9916-88-836-0
ISBN PAPERBACK: 978-9916-88-837-7

# Timeless Tendrils

In shadows deep where whispers play,
The tendrils of time gently sway.
They weave our dreams in subtle light,
And dance with stars that grace the night.

Memories like echoing streams,
Flow softly through our waking dreams.
Each moment caught in nature's grasp,
A fleeting touch, a tender clasp.

The past and present intertwine,
In every heartbeat, every line.
Time's gentle hand will never cease,
In timeless tendrils, we find peace.

As seasons change and ages pass,
We find our strength within the mass.
For in this web of love and fate,
We'll find forever, never late.

# The Portal to Possibility

At dawn's first light, a door appears,
It whispers softly, calms our fears.
A portal wide to dreams unknown,
Where seeds of hope are gently sown.

With every step, the journey starts,
Unraveling the hidden arts.
Each choice we make, a path unfolds,
In realms of wonders yet untold.

The colors swirl, the visions dance,
Inviting us to take a chance.
In this embrace, we redefine,
The essence of our grand design.

So dare to leap, to reach the sky,
For in this space, our spirits fly.
The portal opens wide, we see,
The endless threads of possibility.

## The Hourglass of Hope

Time trickles down, like grains of sand,
Each moment counts, a soft command.
In the silence of dreams, our hopes ignite,
Lighting the dark, like stars at night.

Winds whisper secrets, tales of the past,
Holding on tight, to memories cast.
Through cracks of despair, a light may seep,
Hold on to your dreams, for they're yours to keep.

## Dreamscapes Unveiled

In the stillness, shadows dance and sway,
Revealing secrets, where lost dreams lay.
A tapestry woven with colors bright,
Guiding the way, through endless night.

Each dream a portal, each thought a song,
Whispers of hope that feel so strong.
Through the mist, visions start to unfold,
The heart's deepest wishes, daring and bold.

# The Cauldron of the Now

Boiling thoughts in a cauldron of time,
Stirring emotions, a rhythm and rhyme.
In the present, we find our truth,
Crafting our fates, igniting lost youth.

With every heartbeat, the past fades away,
Adventure awaits in the light of the day.
Embrace this moment, let worries dissolve,
In the cauldron of now, together we'll evolve.

# A Serenade of Shadows

In twilight's embrace, shadows softly sway,
Singing a lullaby, leading astray.
Echoes of whispers, haunting the night,
Guiding lost souls to find their light.

Within the dark, beauty takes flight,
A serenade woven, with stars so bright.
In the folds of silence, we feel the sway,
Embracing the shadows, we dance away.

## Echoes of the Extraordinary

In shadows deep, whispers call,
Colors dance, transcending all.
Dreams ignite in twilight's fade,
Moments born, never betrayed.

Silent stars blink in the night,
Guiding paths with gentle light.
Ancient tales in the breeze,
Carried forth with such ease.

## Serendipity in Stillness

Amidst the calm, a secret waits,
Time holds still, as fate creates.
With every breath, magic flows,
Life in whispers gently grows.

A leaf descends, a quiet sign,
In stillness, hearts begin to shine.
Cascading thoughts like streams do weave,
In each pause, we learn to believe.

## Glimmers of the Unseen

Within the dark, glimmers gleam,
Hints of life within a dream.
Each shimmer speaks of worlds untold,
In shadows, mysteries unfold.

A touch of light on silent ground,
In hidden places, hopes abound.
We chase the echoes of the rare,
Finding beauty everywhere.

# Transient Spells

Moments fleeting, time does sway,
Casting spells along the way.
With every breath, a chance to see,
The dance of life, wild and free.

Softly whispered, secrets shared,
In borrowed time, all are bared.
Each tick, each tock, a precious gift,
In transient magic, spirits lift.

## A Glimpse into Infinity

Stars whisper secrets at night,
Galaxies dance in soft light.
Time stretches beyond what we know,
An endless flight, a cosmic show.

In the silence, dreams take flight,
Boundless visions in twilight.
Each heartbeat echoes through space,
A universe's warm embrace.

Eons pass, and still we gaze,
Lost in the cosmic maze.
The vastness calls us to explore,
Infinity waits, forevermore.

# The Color of a Smile

A smile can light the darkest day,
It paints the world in vivid array.
Joy dances like leaves in the breeze,
Filling hearts with gentle ease.

A curve that brightens the toughest fight,
Bringing warmth like morning light.
Each grin a brushstroke, pure and wide,
A kaleidoscope where hopes reside.

In laughter's echo, we find our way,
Through every shade, the colors play.
Simple moments, a joyous spree,
The brilliant hue of harmony.

## Notes from the Now

In the present, stories unfold,
Moments fleeting and yet bold.
Each heartbeat a note in time's song,
Reminding us where we belong.

The rustle of leaves tells of change,
Life's canvas, vast and strange.
Every breath a chance to feel,
The beauty of what is real.

Listen closely to the day's sigh,
As the sun dips low in the sky.
In every whisper, time can pause,
Notes of life, a sweet applause.

## Magic in the Mundane

In the common, magic lies,
Found in starlit, open skies.
A gentle breeze, a child's laugh,
Moments carved, a sacred path.

In morning coffee, warmth resides,
In laughter shared, true joy abides.
Each simple task, a chance to see,
Wonders hidden, joy's decree.

The quiet hours offer grace,
A chance to slow, to embrace.
In everyday, the heart expands,
Magic flourishes in our hands.

## Illuminated Instants

Moments flicker like stars,
Glimmers of truth in the dark.
Caught between breaths and time,
Life's poetry leaves its mark.

In the hush of the night,
Whispers dance in soft light.
Every sigh holds a tale,
Hidden dreams take their flight.

With each heartbeat we trace,
The spark of a fleeting grace.
Captured by the now, we feel,
Time's gentle, warm embrace.

Fragments of joy unfold,
In colors vivid and bold.
Each instant a gift we cherish,
In memories carefully told.

## The Space Between Sounds

Silence wraps the air tight,
Where echoes dare to reside.
In the pause, magic dwells,
Harmony flows like the tide.

Notes drift like autumn leaves,
Spiraling through the cool breeze.
Moments weave in the quiet,
In the stillness, it all breathes.

Each silence holds a song,
Yearning to find where it belongs.
Between heartbeats, we listen,
To the whispers of our throngs.

In this space, dreams are born,
A canvas yet to be worn.
Melodies linger unplayed,
Till the dawn of a new morn.

# Embracing the Ethereal

In twilight's soft embrace,
We dance on shadows of grace.
The unseen wraps around us,
In a delicate, warm lace.

Glimmers of a world unknown,
Where the spirit finds its home.
We wander through starlit paths,
In the glow of cosmic chrome.

Each breath a fleeting wish,
Carried forth on stardust's swish.
Floating through the mystic air,
In dreams, we taste the bliss.

With every step we take,
The veil of reality shakes.
In the realm beyond the known,
The heart's longing awakes.

# Whims of the Universe

Stars twinkle like soft sighs,
Guiding lost souls through the skies.
In the dance of chaos and calm,
Fate weaves dreams with gentle ties.

Galaxies pirouette in space,
Holding time in a warm embrace.
Every heartbeat echoes loudly,
In the cosmic, boundless race.

Whispers from the distant past,
In the universe, vast and vast.
Moments collide, diverge and play,
In a symphony unsurpassed.

Together, we ride the waves,
Of whims that the stardust gave.
In the quiet of the night sky,
We find the paths our hearts crave.

# The Poetry of Pause

In silence, thoughts take flight,
Moments linger, soft and light.
A breath held in quiet grace,
Time slows down, a gentle space.

Whispers weave through still air,
Hearts find comfort, thoughts laid bare.
Each heartbeat sings the song of now,
In the pause, we learn to bow.

Life unfolds, a canvas wide,
In the stillness, dreams abide.
Nature's rhythm, a calming flow,
In every pause, our spirits grow.

So let us cherish every beat,
In the quiet, life is sweet.
With every moment held so close,
We find the poetry we love the most.

# Raindrops of Bliss

Gentle droplets kiss the ground,
A symphony, a joyful sound.
Nature dances, leaves delight,
As raindrops fall in soft twilight.

Each bead glistens, pure and free,
A fleeting touch of ecstasy.
Running streams and puddled play,
In the rain, we cast away.

Clouds embrace the earth anew,
Painting skies in every hue.
In each drop, a story weaves,
As nature whispers, and time believes.

Raindrops of bliss, a sweet refrain,
Bringing life to every lane.
In their dance, we find our peace,
In the rain, our cares release.

## Luminous Echoes

In twilight's grasp, shadows blend,
Whispers of light around the bend.
Echoes shimmer, soft and bright,
Guiding souls in gentle night.

Stars awaken, dreams take flight,
Painting skies with dots of light.
Each twinkle tells a tale untold,
Of love and warmth, both brave and bold.

Moonlit pathways, silver streams,
Where hopes ignite and fill our dreams.
In the distance, a soft refrain,
Luminous echoes call our name.

So take a step, let shadows play,
In the glow of night, we find our way.
With every echo, a promise glows,
In radiant whispers, our spirit flows.

# Dappled Sunbeams

Through the branches, light cascades,
Golden patterns softly played.
Dappled sunbeams touch the ground,
In warm embrace, beauty found.

Nature's quilt in hues so bright,
Every leaf a source of light.
In the forest, joy reveals,
In dappled dreams, the heart heals.

Children laugh beneath the trees,
Chasing shadows with the breeze.
Sunlight dances, spirits soar,
In each ray, we seek for more.

So let us wander, hearts unchained,
In the wonder, we remain.
Dappled sunbeams, love's caress,
In their glow, we find our rest.

# Shadows of Serendipity

In the quiet hush of night,
Whispers weave through soft moonlight.
Footsteps led by chance and fate,
Hearts entwined, they gently wait.

Dreams dance lightly on the breeze,
Echoes of laughter through the trees.
Every glance a spark ignites,
Guiding souls on starry nights.

Moments caught in fleeting time,
A melody, a whispered rhyme.
Together they embrace the dawn,
In shadows where true love is drawn.

Fate paints paths in secret ways,
A tapestry of vibrant days.
In serendipity's warm embrace,
They find their home in time's sweet grace.

# Captured in Twilight

As the sun dips low in the sky,
Colors blend and softly sigh.
Golden hues and deepening blue,
A perfect canvas, night anew.

The stars awaken, twinkling bright,
Guiding dreams into the night.
Whispers lingering on the air,
Hidden secrets everywhere.

Time stands still in this embrace,
Captured moments, tender grace.
Hearts collide in twilight's glow,
In each pulse, the love will grow.

Underneath the fading light,
They share promises alight.
In every glance, a world unfolds,
Captured in twilight, stories told.

## A Canvas of Wishes

Brush strokes paint the skies above,
Each hue whispers tales of love.
Dreams take flight on colors bold,
In a canvas, wishes unfold.

Stars are scattered like fine sand,
Ocean's waves kiss the golden strand.
Every wish a whispered plea,
Carried forth by destiny.

With each stroke, the heart reveals,
Hopes and dreams, the spirit heals.
Imaginations take their flight,
In this artwork, hearts ignite.

A masterpiece of endless dreams,
Flowing softly like gentle streams.
A canvas woven from the heart,
Each wish a brushstroke, a work of art.

# When Time Dances

In the silence of the night,
Time begins its graceful flight.
Moments twirl, and shadows sway,
Whispers of joy guide the way.

Every heartbeat keeps the pace,
In the rhythm, a warm embrace.
Dancing slowly, lost in bliss,
Time entwined in every kiss.

Around and around, they move,
Finding steps in love's sweet groove.
Eternity in fleeting seconds,
Where every glance is a beacon.

As stars above begin to gleam,
Time dances on, a gentle dream.
In this waltz, they sway as one,
When time dances, hearts are spun.

## A Canvas of Illuminated Time


Brush strokes dance on the edge of night,
Colors bleed in the fading light.
Moments captured, forever spun,
Time unfurls, a tale begun.

Whispers of ages in each hue,
Timeless dreams in shades of blue.
Every layer a story to tell,
In this silence, magic fell.

Stars are painted with silver glimmer,
Horizons stretch, the lights grow dimmer.
On this canvas, hope entwines,
A universe where time aligns.

In every shadow, a secret gleams,
A journey woven in silent dreams.
With each stroke, our hearts entwine,
A canvas filled with love divine.

## Secrets in the Twilight

In the hush of fading day,
Whispers gather, shadows sway.
Secrets linger in the breeze,
Underneath the ancient trees.

Stars awaken, softly gleam,
Carving silence into dream.
Each moment wrapped in mystery,
Twilight holds its history.

Beneath the veil, a world concealed,
In the dusk, truths revealed.
Eyes wide open, hearts will race,
In twilight's grip, we find our place.

Echoes of night, softly call,
Inviting wonder, one and all.
In the twilight, we will fade,
Secrets in the dusk displayed.

# Breath of the Infinite

In the stillness, time unfolds,
Whispers of the universe, bold.
Each heartbeat echoes through the night,
A gentle pulse of ancient light.

In the vastness, we are entwined,
A tapestry of the undefined.
Moments weave like threads of dreams,
In the silence, existence beams.

Across the cosmos, love will soar,
Every breath opens a door.
In the infinite, we find our way,
An eternal dance where shadows play.

With each sigh, the stars align,
In the void, your soul is mine.
Together we breathe, we transcend,
In the infinite, there is no end.

## Stardust Conversations

In the silence of the night, we speak,
Words like stardust, soft and meek.
Glimmers of thoughts in the cosmic glow,
In whispers shared, our spirits flow.

Conversations dance on comet tails,
In the tapestry of celestial trails.
Thoughts adrift in the astral sea,
Boundless echoes are wild and free.

Every twinkle holds a tale,
Secrets written in the stellar veil.
In the quiet, galaxies sigh,
Bridging worlds, you and I fly.

Stardust scattered in a gentle stream,
Cradling hopes, igniting dreams.
With every spark, our hearts ignite,
In stardust, we find our light.

## Whispers of Enchantment

In a forest of dreams, soft shadows play,
Gentle winds carry secrets, night and day.
Moonlight weaves through branches like a fine thread,
Whispers of enchantment, where magic is spread.

Beneath the starlit sky, old tales awake,
Echoes of laughter, each heartbeat they make.
Mysteries linger, hidden from view,
In this tranquil realm, where the night feels new.

With every soft rustle, the heart takes flight,
Dancing with fireflies, in shimmering light.
The air is thick with wishes, hopes that there grow,
In the whispers of enchantment, the spirits flow.

Time drifts on softly, like a dream in the breeze,
Where every breath taken brings infinite ease.
In this sacred space, our souls intertwine,
Bound by the magic, divine and benign.

# Fleeting Starlight

Across the night sky, the stars begin to gleam,
Fleeting moments captured, like whispers in a dream.
Each sparkle a story, yet to be told,
In the silence of time, their secrets unfold.

The velvet darkness wraps the world in peace,
While twinkling lights promise a sweet release.
With each rising dawn, they fade from our sight,
But the heart holds their glow, a warm, gentle light.

In the dance of the cosmos, we sway and glide,
Finding solace in knowing they are our guide.
Though fleeting their presence, their essence remains,
In the memories cherished, the joy and the pains.

So we gaze at the heavens, with wonder anew,
Finding hope in the night, where dreams come true.
For even as starlight slips away from our grasp,
In the tapestry of life, their beauty will last.

## The Dance of Hidden Wonders

In the garden of silence, wonders reside,
Secrets awash in the morning's bright tide.
Petals unfurling, a soft, sweet embrace,
The dance of hidden wonders, a delicate grace.

Glimmers of color bewitch the eye,
Dancing like butterflies, under the sky.
Nature hums softly, a mystical tune,
While shadows waltz freely, beneath the bright moon.

Every leaf tells a tale, each whisper a song,
Together they gather, where dreams may belong.
In the heart of the stillness, joy plays its part,
The dance of hidden wonders ignites the heart.

So step lightly, dear friend, through this vibrant scene,
Unravel the magic where the unseen has been.
In every moment cherished, let your spirit soar,
For the dance of hidden wonders opens the door.

# Flickering Dreams

In the twilight's embrace, soft shadows unwind,
Flickering dreams whisper, leaving trails behind.
They bob and they weave, like a candle's warm glow,
Inviting us softly, where mysteries flow.

Each flicker a promise, a chance to explore,
The realms of our hopes, where our spirits can soar.
Through silken tapestries of thought, we drift wide,
Flickering dreams call us, with arms open wide.

Night wraps around, like a comforting cloak,
Carrying memories, each breath a bespoke.
In the stillness, we wander, hearts wild and free,
Flickering dreams paint the night's reverie.

So hold fast to each moment, let wonder take flight,
For dreams flicker close in the soft, shimm'ring night.
With every heartbeat, let yourself gleam,
As we dance through the whispers of flickering dreams.

# Flickering Fancies

In the dusk where shadows weave,
Dreams awaken, hearts believe.
Whispers dance on velvet breeze,
Echoes of a night that frees.

Candles flicker in the night,
Casting tales of soft delight.
Each small flame a fleeting thought,
Capturing what time forgot.

Memories unravel like thread,
Stories waiting to be said.
Stars above in silent flight,
Guide the seekers of the light.

Fleeting moments, bright and rare,
Hold them close with tender care.
For in fancies, truths are spun,
Life's sweet dance has just begun.

# Chronicles of the Unseen

In shadows deep where echoes play,
Whispers weave through night and day.
Tales of love and grief reside,
In the silence, secrets hide.

Ghostly figures roam the night,
Carving pathways, soft and bright.
Faintest traces left behind,
In the heart, we seek and find.

Starlit paths from past to now,
Ethereal, we take a bow.
Chronicles in twilight penned,
In the dark, our souls extend.

Unseen threads connect us all,
Through the shadows, we will fall.
Every silence breathes a song,
In the unseen, we belong.

# Where Time Stands Still

In the garden, shadows play,
Moments counted, slip away.
Beneath the boughs of ancient trees,
Time finds pause, inviting ease.

Every petal, every leaf,
Holds a tale of joy and grief.
In the stillness, we can rest,
In this space, we feel our best.

Time drips down like morning dew,
In this moment, I see you.
Memories entwined like vines,
In the stillness, life aligns.

Here, the clock's hands cease to move,
In this quiet, hearts can soothe.
Where the seconds hold their chill,
In this haven, time stands still.

## The Kaleidoscope of Now

In a world that spins and sways,
Colors blend in bright displays.
Moments shift like grains of sand,
In this dance, we understand.

Patterns form, then fade away,
Each new twist a fresh bouquet.
Life unfolds in vibrant hues,
Painting joy and hidden blues.

Turn the lens, behold the light,
Every angle sparks delight.
Through the chaos, beauty glows,
In this kaleidoscope, love flows.

Here and now, we take our stand,
Hand in hand, we weave our strands.
In the tapestry of sighs,
Life's rich colors mesmerize.

## Intermissions of Awe

In quiet corners, shadows dance,
Whispers of wonder, a fleeting glance.
Nature breathes in serenity,
Moments wrapped in purity.

Clouds drift gently across the sky,
As trees sway softly, a lonesome sigh.
The sun spills gold on morning dew,
A tapestry woven, fresh and new.

Hearts embrace the calm of night,
Stars awaken, the world's delight.
In every pause, beauty found,
Life's interlude, profound, unbound.

# Flickers of the Extraordinary

A child's laughter echoes near,
In every giggle, joy sincere.
Magic lingers in simple sights,
A world aglow with vibrant lights.

Raindrops tap a whispered tune,
Under the watchful, silver moon.
Petals fall like secrets shared,
Life's flickers show how much we cared.

Together we chase the fleeting muse,
Lost in dreams, we cannot refuse.
In fleeting moments, truths ignite,
Extraordinary hidden in plain sight.

## Tapestry of the Transient

Time weaves tales on fragile threads,
Each second a memory that gently spreads.
Moments blend like colors bright,
Crafting a quilt of day and night.

Echoes linger in the evening breeze,
Soft reminders of life's sweet tease.
Beneath the stars, we find our place,
In patterns woven with subtle grace.

Fleeting shadows, sunshine's kiss,
Every heartbeat, a moment's bliss.
Life's tapestry, ever changing hue,
Transient beauty, forever true.

# A Moment's Alchemy

Transform the mundane into the grand,
Where fleeting seconds draw us close at hand.
In silence, a spark ignites the soul,
A moment of magic that makes us whole.

Glistening dew on morning grass,
Transitory glimmers that cannot pass.
With every breath, the universe sways,
Alchemy unfolds in brilliant ways.

Time melts softly as laughter unfolds,
Molding us gently, the brave and the bold.
Every heartbeat, a potion rare,
Crafting memories in the open air.

## The Breath Between Heartbeats

In the quiet of the night,
Stillness cloaks the weary soul.
Between heartbeats, life takes flight,
Moments linger, time feels whole.

Echoes whisper, soft and low,
In the pause, a secret lies.
Gentle rhythms ebb and flow,
Love is found in silent sighs.

Dreams weave softly through the dark,
Carving paths through shadowed fears.
In the silence, there's a spark,
Binding hearts through all the years.

So breathe deep, and let it be,
In every heartbeat, feel the grace.
For in this space, we find the key,
To cherish life in its embrace.

# A Symphony of Sparks


In the night sky, stars collide,
Creating music, bright and grand.
Each twinkle holds a story wide,
A dance that sings, both bold and planned.

Melodies rise on whispered winds,
Carving notes through vast expanse.
With every burst, the cosmos spins,
A symphony in a cosmic dance.

Crickets chirp their soft refrain,
While fireflies etch their glowing tales.
Harmony flows through joy and pain,
Life's sweet song in every trail.

Join the chorus, feel the zest,
For in each spark, there lies a dream.
A tapestry, life's blessed quest,
In this grand song, we all redeem.

# Threads of Wonder

In a world where colors blend,
Threads of wonder weave and swirl.
Each moment, a new tale to send,
A tapestry of life unfurl.

Gentle whispers call us near,
Curiosity ignites the flame.
In every corner, something clear,
The art of seeing, the joy of the game.

Nature's brush paints every hue,
With strokes of brilliance, wild and free.
In the vastness, visions accrue,
Connecting hearts in unity.

So follow where the wonder leads,
Through winding paths of chance and fate.
For in each thread, a spirit breeds,
Life's rich fabric, we celebrate.

# The Luminous Hush

In twilight's glow, the world exhales,
Shadows dance in soft embrace.
A luminous hush that never fails,
To cradle dreams in time and space.

Stars awaken, gentle and bright,
Each a beacon, a whispered call.
In the silence, there shines a light,
One that beckons, inviting all.

Moonbeams drape the sleeping trees,
Paving paths of silvered grace.
In this moment, hearts find peace,
A sanctuary, a sacred place.

So linger where the hush resides,
In the folds of night, let us trust.
For in this stillness, love abides,
In the luminous hush, we must.

# The Secret Between Breaths

In the quiet space we find,
Whispers of the heart unwind.
Time slows down, a gentle tease,
Lost within the softest breeze.

Moments linger, shadows play,
Secrets in the light of day.
Every sigh a world unknown,
In silence, truth is softly sown.

Feel the stillness, draw it near,
Every breath, a tale to hear.
Between the beats, love will glow,
In the hush, we'll learn to grow.

Hold the calm, a treasure rare,
In this space, we'll shed our care.
The secret lives in gentle streams,
Where every breath is woven dreams.

# Chasing Fireflies

Underneath the velvet sky,
Dancing lights begin to fly.
Childhood laughter in the night,
Chasing dreams in fleeting light.

Fingers reach for glowing trails,
Whispers of enchanted tales.
Moments caught in jars of glass,
Memories that never pass.

In the dark, the world is bright,
Every spark ignites delight.
With each flicker, hearts will soar,
Finding magic, asking for more.

Time stands still in gentle grace,
As we run through time and space.
Chasing fireflies, side by side,
In the glow, our dreams abide.

# Echoes of Enchantment

In the forest, voices call,
Echoes dance through the tall.
Nature sings in vibrant hues,
Every leaf, a tale imbues.

Whispers carried on the breeze,
Secrets shared among the trees.
In the dusk, the shadows blend,
Here, the magic knows no end.

Moonlit paths and starlit skies,
Every twinkle softly sighs.
Enchanting melodies arise,
In the night, our spirits rise.

Beneath the canopy of dreams,
Life is woven into seams.
Echoes linger, softly fall,
In this realm, we hear it all.

## Secrets in Stillness

In the morning's quiet glance,
Moments breathe, a soft romance.
Nature pauses, time does too,
In stillness, we find what's true.

Hidden thoughts in silence bloom,
Whispers carried through the room.
In the depths of gentle calm,
Every secret, sweet as balm.

Endless skies and rolling hills,
Nature's breath, a tranquil thrill.
Listen close to heartbeats sound,
In this still, our peace is found.

In the hush, our spirits meet,
Each soft sigh, a rhythm sweet.
Secrets linger, softly pressed,
In the stillness, we are blessed.

# Surreal Serenades

In twilight's grasp, shadows play,
Soft whispers drift, night turns to day.
Clouds adorned with dreams of gold,
Beneath the stars, secrets unfold.

Chasing flickers of fleeting light,
The moonlit dance, a thrilling sight.
Each note a splash of vivid hue,
In this realm where wishes come true.

Echoes of laughter, the wild breeze,
Cascading thoughts, a gentle tease.
On painted skies, our hearts align,
In surreal serenades, love entwines.

As dawn approaches, visions blur,
Reality bends where dreams occur.
With every breath, we lose control,
In this embrace, we find our soul.

## The Flare of a Lost Minute

Time trickles like sand in glass,
Moments flicker, destined to pass.
A heartbeat stolen, a breath in flight,
Captured in the flare of twilight.

Fleeting shadows stretch and sway,
Whispers of what we wish to say.
In the silence, memories ignite,
A shimmer found in the fading light.

What was once bright, now feels so far,
An instant lost, like a fallen star.
Holding tight to fragments, we pine,
For the flare of a moment divine.

As sunset lingers, dreams take flight,
Embracing the warmth of the night.
In this dance, we find anew,
The precious seconds we clutch, so few.

# Illuminated Echoes

In silent halls where echoes dwell,
Past whispers, stories we cannot tell.
Light glimmers softly on time's old face,
In illuminated corners, we find grace.

Each flicker of flame tells tales untold,
Of love, of loss, and dreams bold.
Memories painted in shades so bright,
Illuminated echoes bring life to the night.

A gentle breeze carries old refrains,
Riding the rhythm of joys and pains.
Through the labyrinth of what's gone by,
These echoes shimmer, never to die.

With every dawn, shadows may fade,
Yet stories linger that time has made.
In illuminated echoes, hearts still race,
Finding solace in this sacred space.

# Shimmering Realities

In a world woven with shimmering threads,
Reality bends, and the ordinary spreads.
Colors collide where dreams take flight,
Transforming the day into vibrant night.

Mirrors reflect what eyes cannot see,
A journey unfolds, wild and free.
Thoughts take shape, a dance of delight,
As shimmering realities twirl in the light.

With each heartbeat, new paths arise,
In the tapestry of whimsical skies.
Laughter echoes from realms unseen,
Crafting moments, serene, pristine.

Together we weave, hand in hand tight,
Building a world where we dare to ignite.
In the fabric of dreams, we find our place,
Shimmering realities, a warm embrace.

# Tapestry of the Present

Threads of time weave in and out,
Moments dance, without a doubt.
Colors blend, vibrant and bright,
Weaving dreams in the soft light.

Echoes of laughter fill the air,
Silent whispers, without a care.
Every second a precious gift,
In this tapestry, spirits lift.

The past a thread, the future gleams,
Now is where we chase our dreams.
In every heartbeat, life anew,
A vibrant world, in every hue.

So let us cherish, hold it near,
The tapestry, woven from cheer.
In the fabric of now, we find our way,
In this moment, we long to stay.

# Luminous Insanity

In twilight's glow, madness sings,
Wild visions take their winged springs.
Fractured thoughts, like scattered stars,
Dance in chaos, heal our scars.

Colors clash, and boundaries blur,
Every whisper a wild stir.
Brilliant colors, a fevered hue,
In this madness, I find you.

Crimson laughter, emerald cries,
Underneath the silver skies.
Every heartbeat thrums with thrill,
In luminous insanity, we spill.

Embrace the wild, let go the tame,
In bright derangement, find your name.
A symphony of strange delight,
In the madness, we take flight.

## Whispers of Wonder

In the quiet of the night,
Soft whispers take their flight.
Stars twinkle with a gentle grace,
Secrets shared in this space.

The moon smiles with a silver beam,
Cradling every wild dream.
Nature sings a tender song,
In the stillness, we belong.

Rustling leaves, a gentle sigh,
Moments flicker as they fly.
Wonder dances in the breeze,
In every rustle, hearts at ease.

So pause, and let your spirit roam,
In whispers of wonder, find your home.
Breathe in deeply, sense the grace,
Magic lives in every place.

## Glimmers in the Gloom

In shadows deep, a spark appears,
Hope glimmers, dissolving fears.
A flicker of light, so pure and bright,
Guides us through the darkest night.

Beneath the weight of heavy skies,
Resilience in our spirit lies.
Every struggle, a shining gem,
In the gloom, we rise again.

Moments small, yet full of grace,
Illuminate this quiet space.
In each heartbeat, courage blooms,
Finding glimmers in the gloom.

So hold the light within your heart,
Even when the world feels dark.
In every shadow, find your theme,
And let your soul forever gleam.

# Elysian Delights

In gardens where the daisies bloom,
The gentle breeze dispels all gloom.
With every petal, joy takes flight,
Illuminating the soft twilight.

Beneath the arch of splendid skies,
Whispers of love, the heart complies.
In laughter shared, the world feels right,
A symphony of pure delight.

Fragrant paths where new dreams tread,
In golden rays, all worries shed.
The taste of honey on the tongue,
Reminds us how the heart is young.

In twilight's clasp, we drift away,
To cherish every vibrant day.
These Elysian gifts we hold tight,
In memories of endless light.

# Evaporating Reveries

In twilight's hush, the shadows play,
Dreams wander softly, drift away.
Each thought dissolves like morning mist,
In the warm glow of dawn's sweet kiss.

The echo of laughter, faint and far,
Fleeting glimpses like a falling star.
Clouds of memories gently sway,
In the realm where dreams decay.

A whisper brushes through the trees,
Carried forth on a tender breeze.
The past released, like grains of sand,
Slips through the fingers of our hand.

In fading light, we close our eyes,
And trace the paths where longing lies.
Those reveries, they rise and fall,
A haunting tale, a wisp, a call.

# Celestial Hues

In a canvas where the stars ignite,
Brushstrokes of colors blend and light.
Twilight drapes in shades of blue,
A cosmic dance, a dream come true.

Each star a wish upon the air,
Celestial whispers beyond compare.
A palette spun with silver threads,
Where hope and wonder softly spreads.

The moon emerges, round and bright,
Guiding hearts through endless night.
In the depths of silence, we find peace,
As cosmic wonders never cease.

These hues of night, so rich and deep,
Invite our souls to wake from sleep.
In celestial realms, we long to soar,
To paint our dreams forevermore.

# Threads of the Fantastic

In tapestries of dreams entwined,
Whispers of magic softly find.
Each thread a story, bright and bold,
A journey waiting to be told.

Through portals of the mind, we roam,
In lands where fantasies call home.
With every stitch, a tale is spun,
Of heroes brave and battles won.

The fabric of night, so richly sewn,
Holds secrets of the unknown.
From realms of wonder, spirits fly,
In threads that weave our dreams up high.

In this tapestry, our hearts embrace,
The threads of life interlace.
In fantastic hues, we shall unite,
In the wonder of the starlit night.

# Captured Wonders

In twilight's grasp, the shadows blend,
A whispered dream where colors wend.
Each petal holds a secret song,
In nature's arms, we all belong.

The stars above begin to play,
As night descends, it veils the day.
In stillness found, our hearts align,
To dance beneath the cosmic sign.

From fleeting moments, joy does bloom,
In every breath, dispelling gloom.
A canvas stretched, horizons wide,
Embrace the wonders that abide.

So let us weave in laughter's thread,
With every step, the path we tread.
As dreams unfold in vibrant hue,
Captured wonders, ever true.

# The Alchemy of Now

In fleeting time, we find our grace,
Moments blend, a soft embrace.
The present sings, a timeless tune,
In every heartbeat, life's fortunes croon.

With every breath, we shape our paths,
Transforming echoes into laughs.
The magic lies in simple things,
In everyday, our spirit springs.

The sun anew, it paints the skies,
With colors bright, our spirits rise.
In every glance, a chance to grow,
The alchemy of now we know.

So hold this moment, let it stay,
In the dance of life, we'll sway.
For in this breath, we find our vow,
Embrace the gift, the alchemy of now.

# Enigmatic Lullabies

Whispers float on moonlit streams,
Where shadows dance and daylight dreams.
In quiet corners, secrets weave,
The lullabies of hearts believed.

Softly sung, the night unfolds,
In every note, a story told.
Beneath the stars, our fears take flight,
Enigmas born from velvet night.

Each melody, a gentle balm,
In every chord, a touch of calm.
The world drifts by with whispered sighs,
In harmony, we find the wise.

So close your eyes, let worries fly,
In lullabies, our spirits lie.
Through shadows deep, we come alive,
In enigmatic whispers, we thrive.

# Radiance in Ordinary Hours

In morning light, the world awakes,
As coffee brews, a stillness breaks.
Each golden ray, a promise made,
In ordinary moments, dreams cascade.

The laughter shared, a simple glance,
In every act, we find romance.
A walk, a word, a fleeting touch,
In daily life, we've found so much.

Through mundane tasks, our spirits soar,
Embracing all the little lore.
In shadows cast, our love is bright,
Radiance blooms in soft daylight.

So celebrate the everyday,
In smallest joys, we're led astray.
For in simplicity, life empowers,
We find our light in ordinary hours.

# Captive Enchantment

In the garden where shadows dance,
A whispering breeze grips my chance,
Petals glisten with morning dew,
A spell unfolds, enchanting too.

Moonlight weaves through ancient trees,
Soft laughter rides upon the breeze,
Time stands still, in velvet night,
Lost in dreams, a wondrous sight.

Twinkling stars in silent grace,
Encircle all in this sacred space,
Captive hearts in twilight's glow,
Love's enchantment starts to grow.

With every breath, a story told,
In whispered secrets, brave and bold,
This fleeting moment, forever held,
In captive enchantment, hearts compelled.

# A Symphony of Fleeting Glimpses

Notes of laughter float in air,
A symphony, both rich and rare,
Moments pass like sparks of light,
Fleeting glimpses, pure delight.

Waves of sound collide and blend,
Each melody a heart to mend,
Echoes dance on autumn's breeze,
Nature's song brings sweet unease.

Chasing shadows, seeking dreams,
Life's a puzzle, bursting seams,
In the silence, whispers rise,
Hidden truths in soft goodbyes.

Gathered memories, warmly held,
In symphonies, our souls are melded,
Every fleeting glance a note,
In this concert, hearts conflate.

## The Sublime Between Heartbeats

In the stillness where time stands still,
Breath and thought begin to thrill,
Moments linger, stretched and sweet,
The sublime lies in the heartbeat.

Between each pulse, a story waits,
Whispers soft from heaven's gates,
In the hush, potential grows,
A thousand worlds in still repose.

Eyes closed tight, the spirit flies,
Floating high in untold skies,
Suspended in this vibrant dream,
Reality's thread begins to seam.

In the space where silence dwells,
Life's greatest secrets, softly tells,
Sublime moments woven tight,
Between heartbeats, purest light.

# Aetherial Encounters

Softly spoken, a voice from afar,
Guides me through the night like a star,
In aether's embrace, spirits sway,
Encounters linger, here to stay.

Subtle brush of a ghostly hand,
In the twilight, we understand,
Wandering souls in timeless space,
Each meeting holds a sacred grace.

Threads of fate, we gently weave,
In starlit dreams, we dare believe,
A dance of shadows, soft and free,
In aetherial realms, just you and me.

Connected by the unseen thread,
Pathways where the heart has led,
These encounters, a timeless waltz,
In the aether, love exalts.

# The Dance of Dawn

The sun peeks over hills,
Golden rays begin to spill.
Birds chirp in sweet delight,
Morning breaks into the light.

Flowers open, colors bright,
Nature dances, pure and right.
Breezes whisper soft and low,
A world awakened, all aglow.

Clouds drift like a gentle stream,
In this moment, we all dream.
Every shadow starts to fade,
In the warmth, new life is made.

With each step, the day is spun,
A brand-new dance has just begun.
Hold this magic close and near,
The dance of dawn is ever dear.

# An Interplay of Light

Sunlight filters through the trees,
Dancing gently with the breeze.
Shadows play upon the ground,
While silence sings without a sound.

Colors merge in soft embrace,
Illumination finds its place.
Nature's palette, rich and wide,
In every corner, dreams collide.

The sky ignites with hues so bright,
As day transitions into night.
Stars awaken, twinkling bright,
In the vastness, soft delight.

Moments blend; time slips away,
An interplay where dreamers stay.
In the twilight's calming grace,
Beauty lives in every space.

# Mosaics of the Infinite

Each star a piece of art divine,
In the cosmos, they align.
Galaxies spin, vast and bold,
Secrets of the night unfold.

Nebulas in colors rare,
Whisper stories through the air.
Time and space, they intertwine,
In the fabric, we define.

Moments captured, etched in light,
Journey through the endless night.
Mosaics made of dreams and fears,
In their beauty, we find tears.

What lies beyond, we cannot know,
Yet in the darkness, sparks still glow.
Infinite wonders call our name,
In this dance of cosmic flame.

## The Sparkle of Stillness

In a moment, time stands still,
Peace enfolds, a gentle thrill.
Quiet whispers, soft and clear,
The heart listens, draws near.

A still pond reflects the skies,
Mirrored dreams where silence lies.
Ripples dance upon the face,
Time holds breath in this space.

Each heartbeat feels the earth's embrace,
In stillness, we can trace.
Every thought, like petals fall,
In the hush, we hear the call.

Let go, and find the spark within,
In stillness, life can truly begin.
A tranquil heart, a lifted soul,
In the quiet, we are whole.

## Dancing on the Edge of Time

In twilight's glow, we spin and sway,
The hourglass whispers of night and day.
Each heartbeat echoes, a silent rhyme,
As we waltz gently on the edge of time.

Moonlight guides us through the dark,
With stars above, they ignite the spark.
In the shadows, we find our prime,
Forever dancing on the edge of time.

Every twirl tells a story untold,
Memories wrapped in silver and gold.
With every step, the world can chime,
In this embrace on the edge of time.

When dawn breaks through, we'll cease our flight,
But the dance lingers in morning light.
In whispers of dreams, we're still in our prime,
Eternally dancing on the edge of time.

# Fragments of the Divine

In the quiet dusk, I find your gaze,
A shimmer of truth in a world of haze.
Each breath a prayer, so pure, so fine,
Collecting the fragments of the divine.

Among the stars, your laughter rings,
A melody woven with angel's wings.
In the stillness, our hearts align,
Embracing the fragments of the divine.

Whispers of hope in a world unknown,
In every heart, there's a seed that's sown.
With every touch, a sacred sign,
We cherish the fragments of the divine.

In twilight moments, we dare to dream,
Beneath the surface, love's gentle stream.
Together we'll rise, forever entwined,
In the dance of fragments of the divine.

# The Quiet Carousel

Round and round on this merry ride,
Colors swirling, worlds collide.
Each horse a wish, each spin a dream,
Life flows quietly, like a gentle stream.

The music plays, a soft refrain,
Whispers of joy, echoes of pain.
Time stands still, yet we must redeem,
The moments lost on the quicksilver beam.

Children's laughter fills the air,
As memories linger with love and care.
Each gentle turn, a chance to gleam,
The beauty found in the quiet carousel.

As we dismount, the magic stays,
In our hearts, it forever plays.
Though life spins on, we find our theme,
In the essence of the quiet carousel.

## Elysian Whispers

Beneath the willow, secrets flow,
Elysian whispers in the soft glow.
Nature's melody, sweet and sublime,
Sings to the heart in poetic rhyme.

Clouds drift lazily across the sky,
As gentle breezes dance and sigh.
Each passing moment, a fleeting mime,
In the embrace of Elysian whispers.

Stars awaken with a radiant gleam,
Inviting us into a wondrous dream.
Boundless thoughts in twilight's clime,
Wrap us softly in Elysian whispers.

With every breath, the world holds still,
In sacred spaces, we bend to will.
Together we'll drift, forever entwined,
Lost in the magic of Elysian whispers.

## A Twinge of Awe

In twilight's soft embrace, we stand,
Whispers of dusk across the land.
Stars flicker like dreams in the sky,
A canvas of wonder, our hearts fly.

Beneath the moon's gaze, shadows play,
Nature's lullaby, night turns to day.
In silence, secrets begin to unfold,
Stories of old in the night so bold.

The breeze carries tales from afar,
Echoes of laughter, each a star.
Life's fleeting moments, we hold tight,
In a twinge of awe, our souls ignite.

## The Essence of Being

In every heartbeat, a truth resides,
An echo of hope where love abides.
Through laughter and sorrow, we find our way,
The essence of being, come what may.

In the still of the morning, life awakens,
Through every challenge, our spirit strengthens.
The world spins gently on this fine thread,
With whispers of dreams that dance in our head.

Connections are forged in the fire of fate,
In every embrace, we cultivate.
Together we rise, together we sing,
In the essence of being, our spirits take wing.

## Heartbeats of Wonder

In the rush of the crowd, a heartbeat calls,
Through crowded rooms where silence falls.
Every gaze holds a tale untold,
Heartbeats of wonder, pure and bold.

With every step on this winding road,
Dreams intertwine, and love is bestowed.
In moments of stillness, we touch the sky,
The world is a canvas, we learn to fly.

In laughter and joy, our spirits rise,
In shared moments, the heart never lies.
Through fleeting time, we dance and sway,
Heartbeats of wonder guide our way.

# The Flicker of Joy

In the early light, the day awakes,
With promises whispered in every breeze that shakes.
The flicker of joy, a spark in the heart,
A moment of magic, a brand new start.

As flowers bloom in colors so bright,
We find our laughter, chasing the light.
Every glance shared, a reason to smile,
In the flicker of joy, we stay for a while.

Through heartaches and trials, we cultivate grace,
Finding beauty and hope in each tender space.
In every heartbeat, life's rhythms align,
The flicker of joy, eternally mine.

# Fleeting Fantasies

Whispers of dreams drift softly by,
Colors dissolve in the evening sky.
Moments blur, like the mist in dawn,
Chasing echoes that quickly are gone.

Fleeting glimpses of worlds so bright,
Glances exchanged in the hush of night.
Hearts race softly, but time won't wait,
In this dance, we tease our fate.

Shadows of laughter, shadows of tears,
Bound by the hopes, entangled fears.
We wander through thoughts, lost in the haze,
Chasing the spark in a fleeting gaze.

Yet here we stand, in this tender glow,
Holding the secrets of what we know.
Tomorrow awaits, with its silent call,
But we'll treasure these fantasies, before they fall.

# The Enchanted Interlude

In the forest where silence sings,
Hidden magic on gossamer wings.
A moment held in the breath of time,
Woven softly into nature's rhyme.

Golden leaves dance in the twilight air,
Transporting us to a realm so rare.
We wander paths where the moonlight spills,
Embracing the quiet, the heart it thrills.

Whispers of ages in the rustling trees,
Carried on melodies, borne by the breeze.
This sacred space, where dreams can flow,
Breathes life into thoughts, igniting the glow.

As the stars awaken, twinkling bright,
We linger on edges between day and night.
Together we dance in this tender embrace,
Finding eternity in this precious place.

# Starlit Reverie

Beneath a sky quilted in silver light,
We chase the shadows of fading night.
Each star a whisper, a tale untold,
Guiding our dreams with their shimmer of gold.

In the hush of twilight, hearts intertwine,
Crafting our secrets, a love so divine.
Mirrors of wonder in your soft, sweet gaze,
Ignite the fire of our starlit daze.

The world fades away; it's just us two,
Wrapped in the glow of indigo blue.
Moments of magic float by like a stream,
Embracing our wishes, igniting the dream.

As constellations twinkle with childhood grace,
We dance together in this timeless space.
Forever enchanted in this celestial sea,
Lost in the wonder of you and me.

# Ephemeral Dreams

In the quiet corners of our minds,
Fleeting visions of love it finds.
Tales woven softly from silken threads,
Whispers of hopes that the heart weds.

Moments like petals that float away,
Fading gently into the light of day.
We grasp at shadows, yet they slip through,
Catching reflections of me and you.

Time paints our dreams in colors so rare,
Sketching the laughter we willingly share.
Yet, like the dawn, they dissolve and break,
Leaving us with whispers in their wake.

Yet in this journey, through joy and strife,
We weave our stories, we craft our life.
And though the dreams may be but a glance,
We'll treasure the moments, embrace the dance.

## Time's Gentle Tickle

Time flows softly, like a breeze,
Whispers of moments, heart at ease.
Each tick a memory, sweet and clear,
Sculpting our laughter, wiping a tear.

A gentle dance of dusk and dawn,
Chasing shadows until they're gone.
With every second, life unfolds,
Stories in silence, quietly told.

The world keeps turning, ever bright,
Embracing the stars that light the night.
In the stillness, find your place,
Where time's gentle tickle leaves a trace.

So cherish each heartbeat, each bright glance,
For in this rhythm lies our chance.
To weave our dreams in threads of gold,
And savor the wonders life has to hold.

## Glowing Horizons

Beneath the arch of skies that gleam,
Awaits the dawn, a waking dream.
Colors explode, a vibrant show,
Painting the earth with fiery glow.

Mountains rise, with peaks of grace,
Under the sun's warm, tender embrace.
Waves of gold kiss the rolling tides,
Where hope and beauty gently collide.

Horizons stretch, where dreams take flight,
Ebbing shadows give way to light.
In every sunrise, a fresh start waits,
Together we'll journey through those gates.

Let visions dance on the edge of night,
Hand in hand, we chase the light.
With open hearts, we face the sun,
In glowing horizons, we become one.

# Flickers of Fortune

A spark ignites in the heart's deep core,
Flickers of fortune, forever soar.
Chance kisses dreams, with luck entwined,
Guiding our paths, by fate designed.

Whispers of hope on the wind do play,
Each moment holds a chance, a sway.
The dice are cast, destiny at hand,
In life's great poker, take a stand.

Some find their treasure in love's embrace,
Others in journeys that time can't erase.
A wink from fortune lights up the night,
Revealing new wonders, a dazzling sight.

So chase the flickers, dance in the glow,
Let fortune guide you, wherever you go.
In the tapestry woven of dreams and fate,
Discover your riches before it's too late.

# Snapshots of Serenity

Captured moments in a tranquil frame,
Snapshots of serenity, never the same.
Whispers of silence, the breeze's soft song,
In stillness we find where we truly belong.

Glimmers of peace in the morning dew,
Nature's embrace, a soothing hue.
Gentle ripples on a calm blue lake,
Reflecting the beauty that silence can make.

A stroll through the meadows, each flower a smile,
Taking a moment to pause for a while.
In the quiet corners where time seems to rest,
We find the treasures that life holds best.

Let each snapshot remind us to breathe,
In the heart's stillness, we weave and weaves.
In the gallery of life, may we always see,
Snapshots of serenity, setting us free.

Milton Keynes UK
Ingram Content Group UK Ltd.
UKHW020656021124
450460UK00007B/61

9 789916 888360